PLESIOSAURS

BY KATE MOENING
ILLUSTRATIONS BY MAT EDWARDS

EPIC

BELLWETHER MEDIA • MINNEAPOLIS, MN

EPIC

EPIC BOOKS are no ordinary books. They burst with intense action, high-speed heroics, and shadows of the unknown. Are you ready for an Epic adventure?

This edition first published in 2023 by Bellwether Media, Inc.

No part of this publication may be reproduced in whole or in part without written permission of the publisher. For information regarding permission, write to Bellwether Media, Inc., Attention: Permissions Department, 6012 Blue Circle Drive, Minnetonka, MN 55343.

Library of Congress Cataloging-in-Publication Data

LC record for Plesiosaurs available at: https://lccn.loc.gov/2022050379

Text copyright © 2023 by Bellwether Media, Inc. EPIC and associated logos are trademarks and/or registered trademarks of Bellwether Media, Inc.

Editor: Betsy Rathburn   Designer: Jeffrey Kollock

Printed in the United States of America, North Mankato, MN.

TABLE OF CONTENTS

WHAT WERE PLESIOSAURS?

PRONUNCIATION

PLEE-zee-uh-SORE

Plesiosaurs were giant **reptiles**. They lived in oceans around the world.

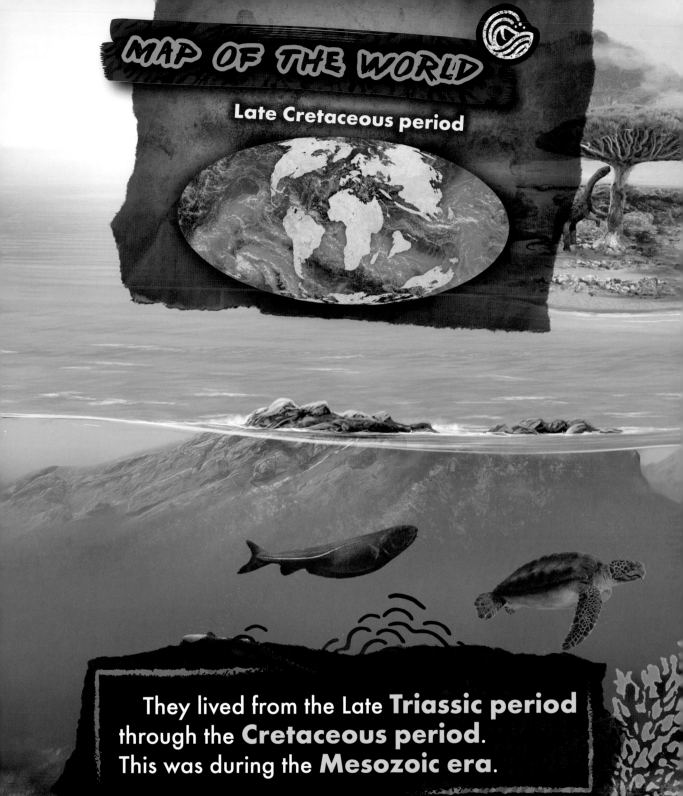

Late Cretaceous period

They lived from the Late **Triassic period** through the **Cretaceous period**. This was during the **Mesozoic era**.

Plesiosaurs could grow over 40 feet (12.2 meters) long. They could weigh nearly 100,000 pounds (45,359 kilograms).

flippers

They had four **flippers**. These helped them swim quickly. They had sharp teeth for catching **prey**.

SIZE COMPARISON

about as long as a semi-truck trailer

There were two types of plesiosaurs.
Some had long necks. Their necks made up
more than half of their body length!

long-necked
plesiosaur

short-necked
plesiosaur

Others had shorter necks. Short-necked
plesiosaurs had bigger heads.

THE LIVES OF PLESIOSAURS

Plesiosaurs were **carnivores**. Long-necked plesiosaurs ate small fish and squids.

They swung their heads back and forth as they hunted. This helped them catch food.

STRAIGHT NECKS

Long-necked plesiosaurs probably had straight necks. This helped them swim faster! But their necks could not bend easily.

ROCK EATERS

Plesiosaurs could not chew well. Some plesiosaurs swallowed rocks! The rocks may have helped mash up food in their stomachs.

Short-necked plesiosaurs were **apex predators**. They were fast, strong swimmers. They attacked prey from below.

These plesiosaurs ate large fish and reptiles. Some even ate other plesiosaurs!

PLESIOSAUR DIET

fish

squids

reptiles

Plesiosaurs gave birth to live young. Some babies stayed with their mothers for years. This helped keep them safe.

Adult plesiosaurs had few enemies.
But babies could be prey for other carnivores.

FOSSILS AND EXTINCTION

asteroid

A large **asteroid** hit Earth about 66 million years ago. This caused big changes to Earth's **climate**.

Plesiosaurs could not survive the changes. They went **extinct**.

The first plesiosaur **fossil** was found in England in the early 1800s. This area used to be underwater.

FIRST FOSSIL

Mary Anning found the first plesiosaur fossil. Many people thought it was fake at first!

fossil

BIGGEST PLESIOSAUR FOSSIL EVER FOUND

plesiosaur fossil

EUROPE

FOUND in 2006

LOCATED Svalbard, Norway

Since then, plesiosaur fossils have been found around the world. Fossils help scientists study the world of the plesiosaur!

GET TO KNOW THE PLESIOSAUR

large body

four flippers

WEIGHT
nearly 100,000 pounds
(45,359 kilograms)

FOOD

fish

squids

reptiles

SIZE over 40 feet (12.2 meters) long

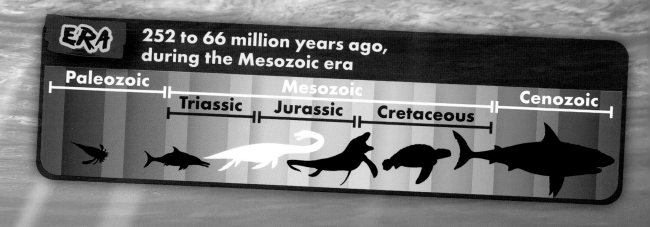

ERA 252 to 66 million years ago, during the Mesozoic era

Paleozoic | Mesozoic | Cenozoic
Triassic | Jurassic | Cretaceous

sharp teeth

LOCATION
oceans around the world

FIRST FOSSIL FOUND
in the early 1800s by Mary Anning

GLOSSARY

apex predators—animals at the top of the food chain; apex predators hunt other animals for food but do not have predators of their own.

asteroid—a rocky object in space that travels around planets or stars

carnivores—animals that only eat meat

climate—the long-term weather in a particular place

Cretaceous period—the last period of the Mesozoic era that occurred between 145 million and 66 million years ago

extinct—no longer living

flippers—flat body parts that are used for swimming

fossil—the remains of a living thing that lived long ago

Mesozoic era—a time in history that happened about 252 million to 66 million years ago; the first birds, mammals, and flowering plants appeared on Earth during the Mesozoic era.

prey—animals that are hunted by other animals for food

reptiles—cold-blooded animals that have backbones and lay eggs

Triassic period—the first period of the Mesozoic era that occurred between 252 million and 200 million years ago

TO LEARN MORE

AT THE LIBRARY

Barker, Chris. *Super Dinosaur Encyclopedia*. New York, N.Y.: DK Publishing, 2020.

Taylor, Charlotte. *Digging Up Sea Creature Fossils*. New York, N.Y.: Enslow Publishing, 2022.

Yang, Yang. *The Secrets of Ancient Sea Monsters: PNSO Encyclopedia for Children*. Dallas, Tex.: Brown Books Kids, 2021.

ON THE WEB

FACTSURFER

Factsurfer.com gives you a safe, fun way to find more information.

1. Go to www.factsurfer.com.

2. Enter "plesiosaurs" into the search box and click 🔍 .

3. Select your book cover to see a list of related content.

INDEX

The images in this book are reproduced through the courtesy of: Mat Edwards, front cover, pp. 1, 2, 3, 4-5, 6-7, 8-9, 10-11, 12-13, 14-15, 16-17, 18-19, 20-21; paleobear/ Wikipedia, p. 19 (fossil); Sedgwick Museum/ Wikipedia, p. 21.